ULTIMATE BEGINNER SERIES®
BLUEGRASS
MANDOLIN *Basics*

by Dennis Caplinger

Cover mandolin courtesy Gibson Guitars.

Alfred Publishing Co., Inc.
16320 Roscoe Blvd., Suite 100
P.O. Box 10003
Van Nuys, CA 91410-0003
alfred.com

ISBN-10: 0-7692-8541-4
ISBN-13: 978-0-7692-8541-2

MW00564275

CONTENTS

INTRODUCTION

This book is designed to help you learn to play the mandolin in the flatpicking bluegrass style. If you are a beginner, that's great—we'll start from scratch and cover all the bases. If you already play a little, that's okay, too—there are some good versions of tunes here, as well as some basic tips on how to play with other people in a band context.

ABOUT THE CD

All of the music examples and tunes in this book are included on the CD. It is very important for you to listen to the music as much as possible in order to really get a feel for the way these tunes are supposed to sound. There is no way to adequately notate all the subtle nuances of this music, so *listen, listen, listen!*

The tunes on the CD are mixed so that the band is on the left side of the stereo field and the mandolin is on the right by itself. By panning the music hard left, the mandolin disappears so that you can be the only mandolin playing along. Panning the music hard right will solo the mandolin so that you can study it in detail without hearing the other instruments. The CD track number is listed at the top of each example for easy reference.

PARTS OF THE MANDOLIN

Headstock

Tuning keys
(pegs)

Nut

Frets

Neck

Soundhole

Pickguard

Bridge

Tailpiece

Strap Button

TUNING THE MANDOLIN

The mandolin has eight strings, tuned in pairs. The two strings in each pair are tuned in "unison," which means both strings are tuned to the same note. To make things easier, we will refer to each of these pairs as a single string, as if the mandolin only had four strings instead of eight. The two lowest strings (both tuned to G) will be called the "4th string." The next pair (tuned to D) will be called the "3rd string." The next pair (tuned to A) will be called the "2nd string." The final pair (tuned to E) will be called the "1st string." When tuning a pair of strings, be careful to pick only one of the strings in a pair—tune that single string and then tune the second string of the pair so that they match perfectly.

Tuning to a Keyboard

The four strings of a mandolin can be tuned to a keyboard by matching the sound of each open mandolin string to the keyboard notes as indicated in the diagram.

Note: You will hear the "intonation" (exact relationship of pitches) better, and your mandolin will stay better in tune, if you loosen the strings and tune them **up** to pitch rather than bringing them from the above pitch and tuning down.

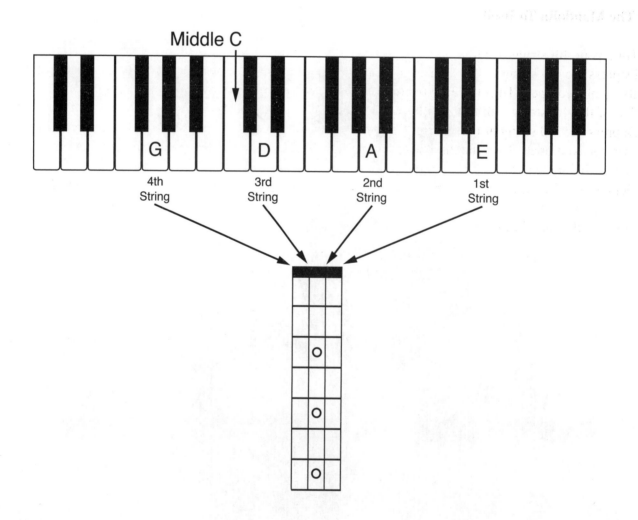

Electronic Tuners

Many brands of small battery-operated tuners are available. These are excellent for keeping your mandolin in perfect tune and for developing your ear to hear intonation very accurately. Simply follow the instructions supplied with the tuner.

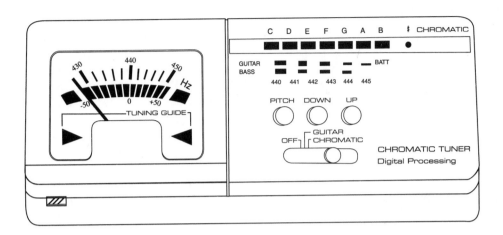

Tuning The Mandolin To Itself

- Tune your 4th string (G) to a piano or some other instrument.
- Depress the 4th string at the 7th fret. Play it and you will hear the note D, which is the same as the 3rd string played open. Turn the 3rd string tuning key until the pitch of the open 3rd string (D) matches that of the 4th string, 7th fret.
- Depress the 3rd string at the 7th fret. Play it and you will hear the note A, which is the same as the 2nd string played open. Turn the 2nd string tuning key until the pitch of the open 2nd string (A) matches that of the 3rd string, 7th fret.
- Depress the 2nd string at the 7th fret. Play it and you will hear the note E, which is the same as the 1st string played open. Turn the 1st string tuning key until the pitch of the open 1st string (E) matches that of the 2nd string, 7th fret.

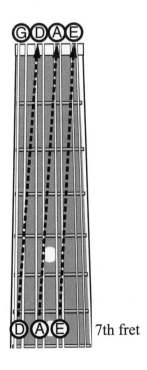

READING THE MUSIC EXAMPLES IN THIS BOOK

Example 1

Here is a sample measure that includes eighth and quarter notes:

The count shown in this example won't appear in every tune, but we will include it in the first few examples in order to give you an idea of how to count time. Each count (number) is equal to one beat (quarter note), and the notes in between fall on "and." The symbols (⊓ and V) refer to the right-hand picking direction:

⊓ = downstroke with flatpick

V = upstroke with flatpick

You will notice that this book includes standard notation along with all of the tablature; this is a significant departure from most other mandolin instructional books. Our rationale for this is that music notation may make the learning process easier for students who are familiar with it or for students who are learning mandolin after already studying another instrument (like piano or violin, for example). For those folks who don't care to learn about or use music notation, that's okay, too. The tablature system is a great way to learn and is actually the most common way to learn to play bluegrass-style mandolin. Using either method along with the enclosed CD will yield good results.

For more in-depth information on music notation and TAB, see the appendices beginning on page 83.

UNIT 1: SOME BASICS

Choosing a Mandolin

There are a few things you'll need to have in order to work your way through this book. First, you need to be playing an acoustic eight-string mandolin. Bluegrass mandolin players use flat-backed, steel-stringed mandolins as a rule (as opposed to round-back classical or Italian mandolins) because the steel strings and large body styles provide the volume and tone necessary for bluegrass. Make sure that the mandolin you're playing is in good condition. I always advise students to have a reputable luthier look at their instruments before they get started. Playing the mandolin is difficult enough without having to fight an instrument that is poorly set up. There are many adjustable parts to a mandolin and, like an automobile engine, if the parts are not adjusted correctly, it won't work properly. Even the most famous players often have their instruments professionally set up, so don't be afraid to have someone look at your mandolin if it needs it.

The Flatpick

You'll be learning to pick the strings using a flatpick. It's okay to start out picking with just your bare fingers, but you should get used to using a flatpick as soon as possible. There are several different brands to choose from, so visit your local music store and see what's available. Picks come in various sizes, colors, materials, and thicknesses. I recommend that you start out using a plastic pick of medium thickness and of the shape shown below. This will help you get the best tone and volume out of your mandolin. Later, as your style and technique develop, you may want to experiment with other pick types and thicknesses. For now, just try to hold your flatpick like mine in these photos:

 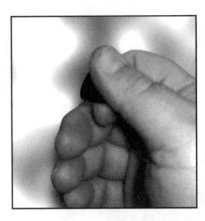

The Strap

Get a strap for your mandolin. Even though you'll probably be learning to pick while sitting, a strap will help you balance the weight of the mandolin and keep you from having to support the neck with your left hand. I like to use a leather strap and attach it to the strap buttons on the mandolin like this:

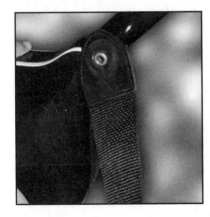 

If your mandolin does not have a strap button at the heel of the neck, you can attach the strap to the peghead like this:

If you have an F-5 body style you can attach the strap to the scroll on the body like this:

Wear the strap over your left shoulder and adjust the length of the strap so that the mandolin sits comfortably and solidly in your lap without slipping. Angle the neck up slightly like this:

Many famous bluegrass mandolin players wear their straps over the right shoulder instead:

The "right-shoulder method" is especially common among first- and second-generation traditional players, and modern players who are patterning their styles after Bill Monroe (and using an F-5 style mandolin). You can try positioning your strap both ways and see which you prefer. One of the most important things to remember about learning to play the mandolin is that everyone's body is different. What may be comfortable for someone else may not be right for you. Try to position the mandolin and your hands so that they approximate the position in the photos you see here.

Right-Hand Position

Place your right hand on the mandolin like this:

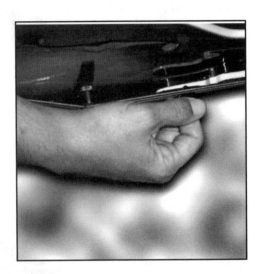

It is very important that you rest the base of the palm of your right hand lightly on the mandolin just on top of the bridge. Be careful not to mute the strings. This can be awkward at first, but it will help to keep your picking hand stable. Avoid anchoring your fingers on the face of the mandolin. Try to keep your hand and wrist relaxed—this will help keep your picking smooth and even.

Left-Hand Position

Place your left hand on the neck of the mandolin like this:

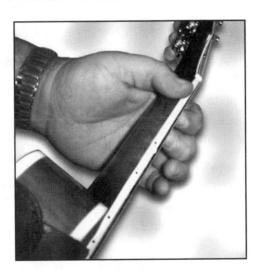

It is important to try to keep the thumb of your left hand on the back of the mandolin neck as shown in the photo above. Resist the temptation to lay the neck in the palm of your hand. Proper left-hand placement will allow you to develop good fingering technique and help build speed.

UNIT 2: BASIC FLATPICKING

THE RIGHT HAND

Our right hand is like our voice. We need to develop the right hand so that it can articulate any notes that we need to play—on any string and in any order. You could say that the right hand is a slave to the left. We'll get started by learning some basic right-hand picking patterns. Learning to play these patterns cleanly and smoothly is the most important part of learning to pick on the mandolin. The best way to practice these patterns is to start very slowly and evenly, playing each pattern over and over many times. Concentrate on counting each beat and try not to speed up or slow down. Remember: speed only comes with practice!

 Example 2: Quarter-Note Downstrokes

Pick each string evenly using only downstrokes. Make sure to keep your right wrist loose and relaxed and count "1, 2, 3, 4."

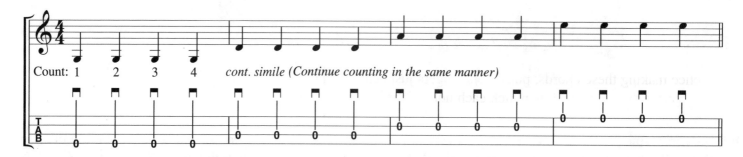

You'll notice in the above pattern that after each downstroke, you have to bring the pick back up in order to position it for the next downstroke. It is possible to strike the string again during this upward movement; we call this an "upstroke." Alternating between downstrokes and upstrokes smoothly and evenly is a vital part of learning to flatpick.

 Example 3: Eighth-Note Downstrokes and Upstrokes Combined—Alternate Picking

Pick each string evenly using a combination of downstrokes and upstrokes. This is called 'alternate picking.' The notes are called eighth notes and are counted "1&2&3&4&." Pay attention to the pick direction symbols. Downstrokes occur on the numbers of the count (1, 2, 3, 4) and upstrokes occur on the '&'s' between the numbers. Take it slowly and count.

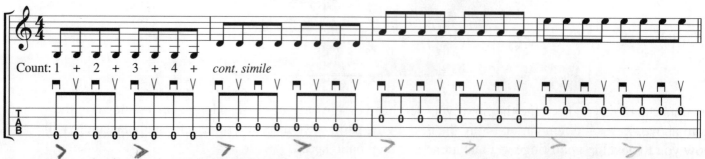

I cannot overemphasize the importance of keeping your downstrokes and upstrokes in the right places. As you are counting, the numbers are always downstrokes and the "&'s" between the numbers are always upstrokes. Developing this back and forth or "alternating" motion of your flatpick will enable you to play quickly and cleanly with the correct accents and timing necessary for bluegrass. Practice these exercises over and over!

LEFT-HAND BASICS

Now that you have some right-hand basics, let's look at a few left-hand chords. (Refer to "chord block diagrams" in Appendix 3 for an explanation of chord frames.) Remember to try to keep your left-hand thumb in the middle of the back of the mandolin neck. Put your left-hand fingers down right behind the appropriate fret as shown in the chord diagrams:

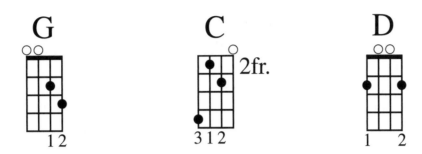

To practice making these chords, place your fingers just behind the appropriate fret and on the correct string as indicated in the diagrams, and then pick each note of the chord individually with your flatpick using a downstroke. Make sure that each individual note rings clear and clean. If the note is muted or buzzing, rearrange your finger position until the note is clear. When all the notes of the chord sound clean, then lightly strum all the strings together with a downstroke. Now practice changing from one chord to another: G to C to D and back to G, over and over until you can change from one to another easily and cleanly. These three chords are the main chords in the key of G and we will use them over and over again.

PUTTING BOTH HANDS TOGETHER

Now that you have a handle on some right- and left-hand basics, let's try putting the hands together so we can begin to make some real music. Remember to take things very slowly at first—it will take awhile to develop coordination between your hands. If you encounter difficulty, go back to practicing the left- and right-hand skills separately; then try putting them together when you feel comfortable. Even the best players sometimes work on the hands separately if they are trying to solve problem areas in their playing.

Example 4: The G Scale

Many of the tunes we will be learning are in the key of G. Let's learn the G scale. While you are trying to learn where the left-hand notes are for this scale, it is okay to use only downstrokes in your right hand. However, when you become familiar with the left-hand fingering, play the scale using alternate picking. Pay close attention to your pick direction. Try to keep the fingers of your left hand arched above the fretboard and your left thumb in the center of the back of the neck. Stay relaxed and loose!

Here is the G scale in the lower octave.

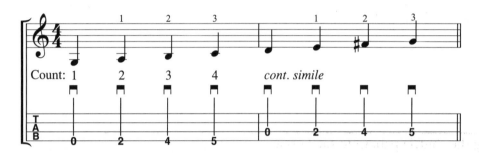

Example 5

Here is the G scale in the higher octave:

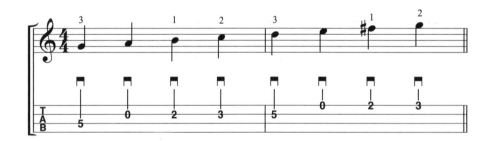

Example 6

Now play the G scale up and back down again over both octaves—watch your pick direction!

14

Example 7: Right-Hand Fiddle Shuffle Pattern

We've played some quarter notes with downstrokes and eighth notes using alternate picking. Now, here's a pattern combining both quarter notes and eighth notes. This is called a "fiddle shuffle" pattern because it creates a rhythm that is often used by bluegrass and old-time fiddlers. We will use it, also. The right-hand pattern can be confusing, so pay close attention to your pick direction. The pick direction for this pattern is down, down, up, down, down, up, etc. The count for this pattern is "1, 2&, 3, 4&" etc. Remember: the numbers are downstrokes, the &'s are upstrokes.

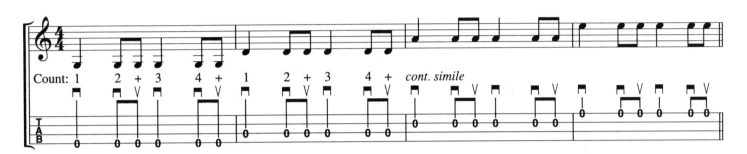

Example 8

Now, let's try applying the shuffle pattern to the G scale.

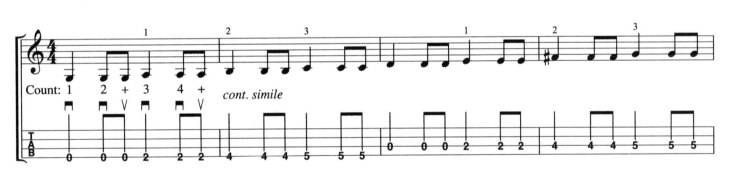

15

Example 9: Boil the Cabbage Down (in G Major)

Now it's time to play our first real song, "Boil the Cabbage Down." This song is an old-time fiddle tune that we'll play with the band later. The right-hand pattern all the way through is the fiddle shuffle.

The **repeat sign** (‖) in the next to last measure indicates to repeat the song back from the beginning. After the second time through, play the second ending and just end; don't repeat again. Once again, take it slow and count.

BOIL THE CABBAGE DOWN
(in G Major)

TRADITIONAL

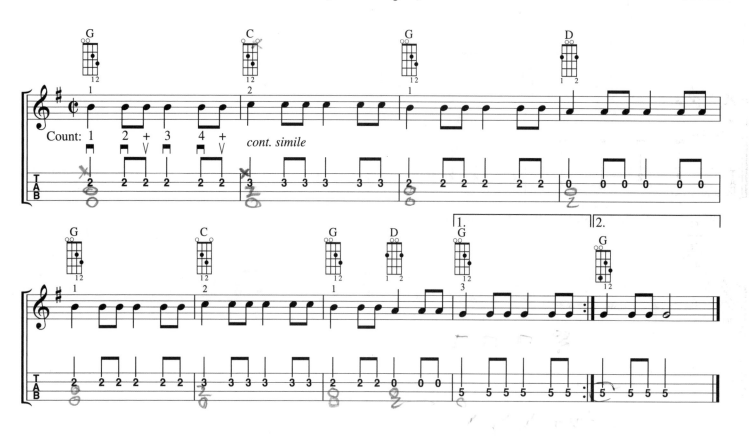

For an explanation of first and second endings, see Appendix 1, pg. 83.

Example 10: Skip to My Lou

Here's another old favorite. Although "Skip to My Lou" is not a bluegrass favorite, it is a good tune to practice because the melody combines both quarter-note and eighth-note patterns—part of it is fiddle shuffle and part is not. Most of the tunes we will learn use a combination of patterns in the right hand instead of just one pattern all the way through. Pay attention to your pick direction and count!

SKIP TO MY LOU

TRADITIONAL

UNIT 3: BASIC BLUEGRASS RHYTHM

One of the most enjoyable things about making music is being able to play with other people. The interaction among the various instruments in a bluegrass band is a big part of what defines the music—that is, what makes it sound 'bluegrass.' Each instrument has a unique role in the band sound, depending on whether it is playing lead or backup. In a typical bluegrass setting, only one of the instruments in the group will be playing a solo at any given time. This is not always true of other forms of music. In Irish music, for example, it is very common for everyone to be playing the melody together at the same time. Learning to play backup is very important when you're in a group setting because, if you are jamming with other pickers and singers, most of your time will be spent supporting other players. You can (and should) spend as much studying the art of playing backup as you spend playing lead. There are many different types of backup, but the single most important skill to learn is how to play good, solid rhythm.

Example 11: Basic Strum

The basic strum pattern involves hitting the bass note of a chord with a downstroke, followed by lightly strumming across the top three strings of the chord with another downstroke. Here is the pattern using a G chord. Count 1, 2, 3, 4.

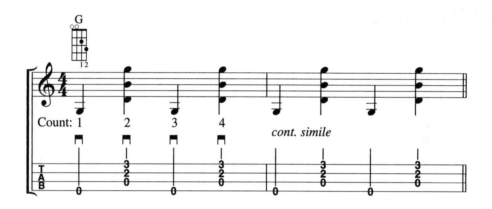

Example 12

Now try the same pattern with a C chord.

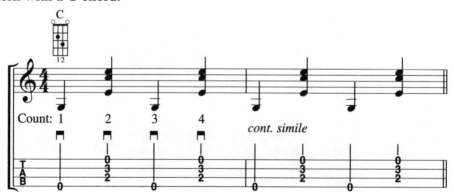

18

Example 13

Here's the pattern with a D chord.

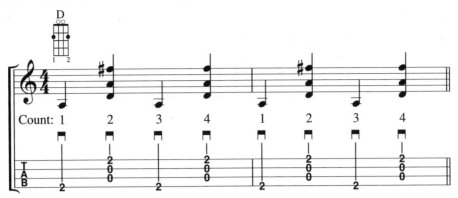

Example 14

Now, try the pattern while changing between chords. Remember to take it slow and count.

Example 15: Using the Fiddle Shuffle as a Rhythm Strum

We can take our rhythm playing a step further now by applying the fiddle shuffle pattern. This is almost like the basic rhythm strum—play the bass note with a downstroke, strum lightly down across the top three strings, but then strum lightly back up across the top two or three strings before hitting the next bass note. Here's the pattern with a G chord. Remember to strum lightly and count 1, 2&, 3, 4&:

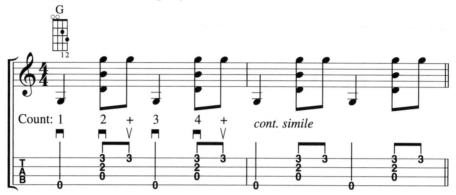

Example 16

Here's the pattern with a C chord.

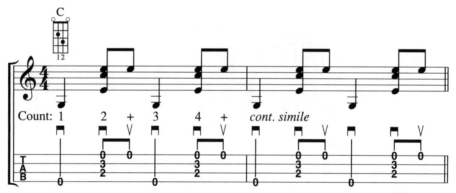

Example 17

And a D chord.

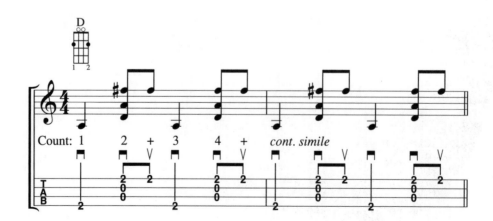

Example 18: Boil the Cabbage Down (chord progression)

Here is the rhythm part or "chord progression" for "Boil the Cabbage Down." This is what we play when the other instruments are soloing or the vocalist is singing—whenever we're not soloing.

BOIL THE CABBAGE DOWN
(Chord Progression)

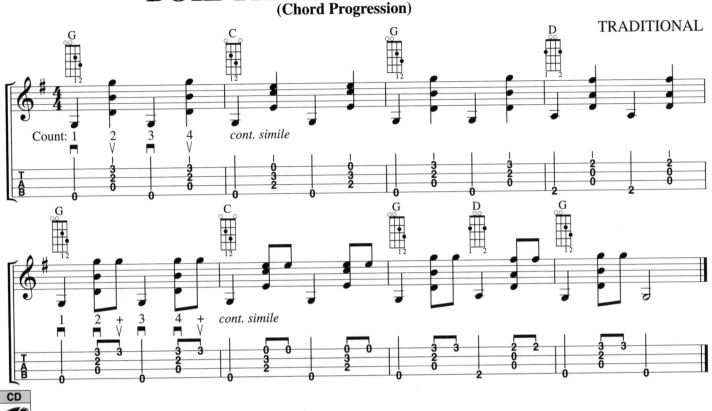

Example 19: Skip to My Lou (chord progression)

SKIP TO MY LOU
(Chord Progression)

Don't forget that you cannot practice the above examples, exercises, and chords too much. Practice, practice, practice! Strive to play evenly and don't forget to count. Sooner or later, you'll develop a sense of timing so that you feel the beat and won't have to count out loud. One excellent exercise is to play a single pattern (like the fiddle shuffle rhythm, for example) over and over for a minute without stopping, concentrating on not missing any of the strings and playing as evenly as possible. If you think a minute isn't a long time, just try it!

The Key of A

Some of the instruments in a bluegrass band—banjo, guitar, and dobro—often use a "capo" (a device for clamping the strings at different fret positions) to play in different keys. The fiddle, bass, and mandolin do not use a capo. To play in a given key on the mandolin, we need to learn the scale and chord positions for that key. Until now, we have been working in the key of G. Let's move on to the key of A, a very common key for bluegrass.

Example 20

Here is the A scale in the low octave.

Example 21

The A scale in the higher octave.

Example 22

And the A scale over both octaves.

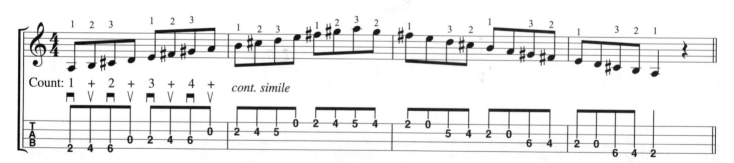

The three main chords in the key of A are A, D, and E. Here is the basic A chord. Place your left-hand index finger across the 3rd and 4th strings at the 2nd fret in order to make this chord—this is called "barring."

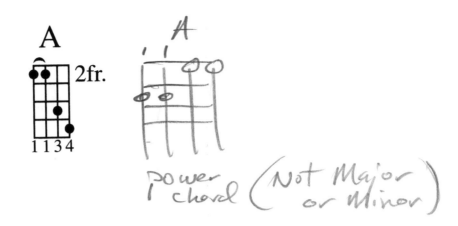

A
2fr.
1 1 3 4

power chord (Not Major or Minor)

Here is the basic D chord.

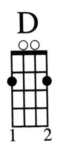

D
○○
1   2

And here is the E chord: barre the 2nd and 3rd strings at the 2nd fret with your left-hand index finger.

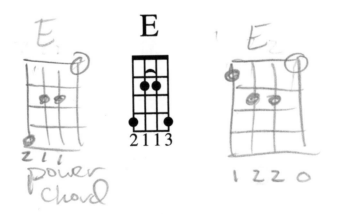

E
2 1 1 3

E — 2 1 1 power chord

E — 1 2 2 0

23

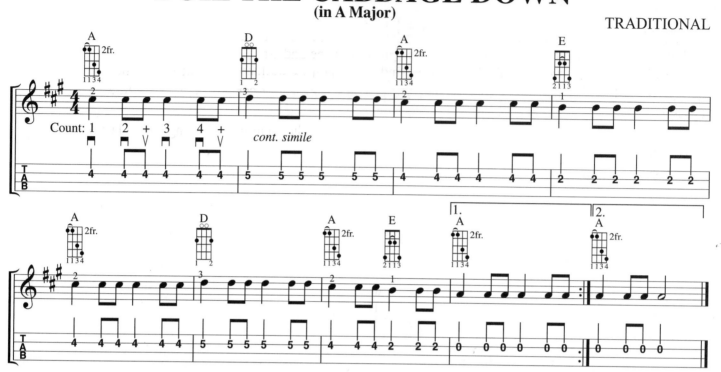

Example 23: Boil the Cabbage Down (in A Major)

Now, let's learn this tune in the key of A, where it is most often played by fiddlers.

BOIL THE CABBAGE DOWN
(in A Major)

TRADITIONAL

Example 24: Boil the Cabbage Down (chord progression in A Major)

BOIL THE CABBAGE DOWN
(Chord Progression in A Major)

TRADITIONAL

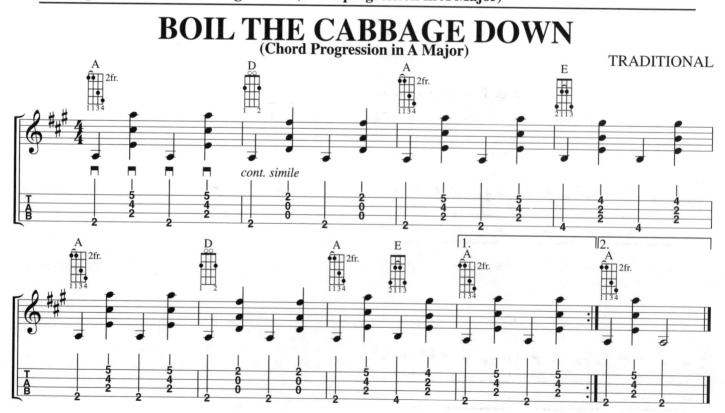

UNIT 4: LEFT-HAND TECHNIQUES

THE SLIDE

Some of the neatest sounds you can make on the mandolin come from the combination of right-hand picking patterns with various left-hand embellishments or ornaments. Many of the characteristic sounds of bluegrass mandolin come from these left-hand techniques, which you can use to make a basic melody more interesting.

 Example 25

Try this: Put the middle finger of your left hand on the 3rd fret of the 2nd string. Pick the string with a right-hand downstroke, and then immediately slide your left hand up the neck so that your middle finger moves from the 3rd to the 4th fret. Keep your middle finger down on the string so you can hear the note "slide" from one pitch to the next. You pick only the first note—the second note is the result of the slide. Notice in the TAB that a slide is notated with a slur mark (pick only the first note) and a diagonal line showing the slide from one note to the next.

 Example 26

This time, we slide from the 6th to the 7th fret on the 3rd string. You can slide on any string, using any finger.

 Example 27: Boil the Cabbage Down (with slides)

Let's use some slides in a tune we already know. Here's another version of "Boil the Cabbage Down" using some slides.

25

THE HAMMER-ON

Example 28

The next left-hand technique we'll look at is the "hammer," or "hammer-on." Get your left hand ready for this technique. Hold the index finger of your left hand over the top of the 2nd fret of the 2nd string, but don't touch it yet. Pick the 2nd string with a right-hand downstroke; then immediately hammer your index finger down onto the 2nd string at the 2nd fret. You pick only the first note; the hammering down of your index finger onto the string sounds the second note. The hammer is used whenever you have an upward slur that is not a slide (play the first note and hammer your finger down on the next note).

Example 29

As with the slide, the object when hammering a note is to get the second note (which is not picked with the right hand) to be as loud as the first note (which is picked by the right hand).

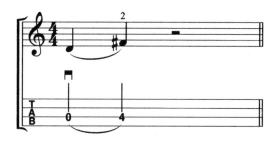

Example 30

Another very common technique is to fret a note with a left-hand finger and then while still holding that note, hammer with a different left-hand finger.

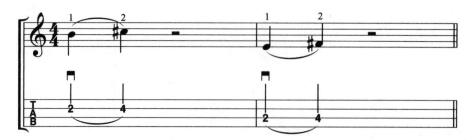

In the previous example, the note on the 2nd fret was held down by the left-hand index finger, and the hammer to the 4th fret was performed by the left-hand middle finger. When you do a hammer like this, the left-hand index finger should remain down on the string even after the middle finger is hammered-on.

26

Example 31

Here are some hammer-on exercises using the fiddle shuffle pattern.

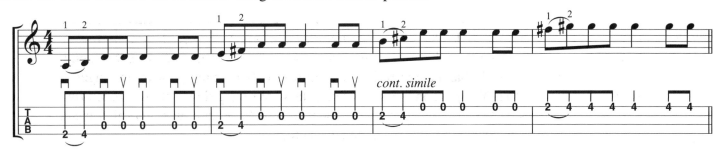

Example 32: Cumberland Gap

Here is a popular bluegrass tune. Watch out for both slides and hammers. Have fun with "Cumberland Gap."

CUMBERLAND GAP

TRADITIONAL

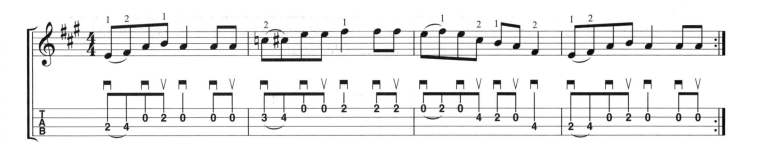

Example 33: Cumberland Gap (chord progression)

CUMBERLAND GAP

(Chord Progression)

TRADITIONAL

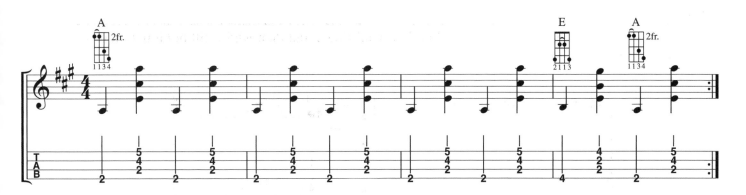

THE PULL-OFF

CD
24A **Example 34**

The pull-off is another technique that you will use a lot. Basically, this technique is the exact opposite of the hammer-on technique. Put your left-hand index finger on the 2nd fret of the 2nd string. Pick the 2nd string with a right-hand downstroke and then immediately snap your left-hand index finger off of the string in the direction of your palm. When done correctly, the second note will be almost as loud and clear as the first note.

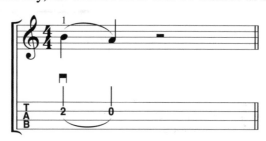

CD
24B **Example 35**

Here are some more pull-offs. *(pluck off)*

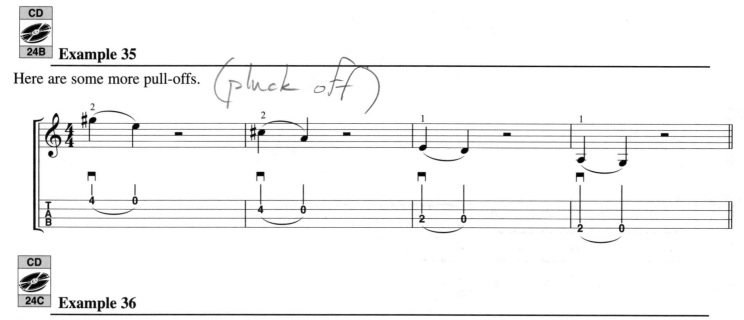

CD
24C **Example 36**

You can also pull-off from one finger to another.

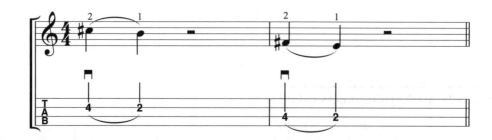

In example 36, the left-hand index finger should be on the 2nd fret and the middle finger should be on the 4th fret of the string at the same time; then pull the middle finger off while leaving the index finger firmly planted on the 2nd fret.

28

Example 37

Examples 37 and 38 are pull-offs combined with some fiddle shuffle and alternate picking patterns.

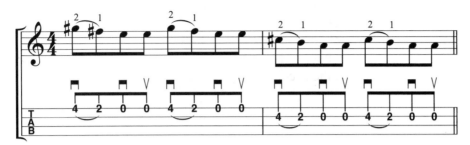

Example 38

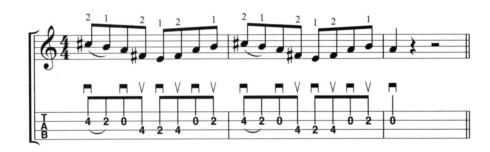

Example 39: Cripple Creek

Now that you have a firm grasp of all three left-hand techniques (the slide, hammer-on, and pull-off), let's try a tune that combines all of them. "Cripple Creek" has a "form" that is very common in bluegrass music and one that we will see over and over again in this book: AABB. The tune has an A section, which is repeated, followed by a B section, which is repeated. Watch for the repeat signs. Remember to watch your pick direction and count.

CRIPPLE CREEK

TRADITIONAL

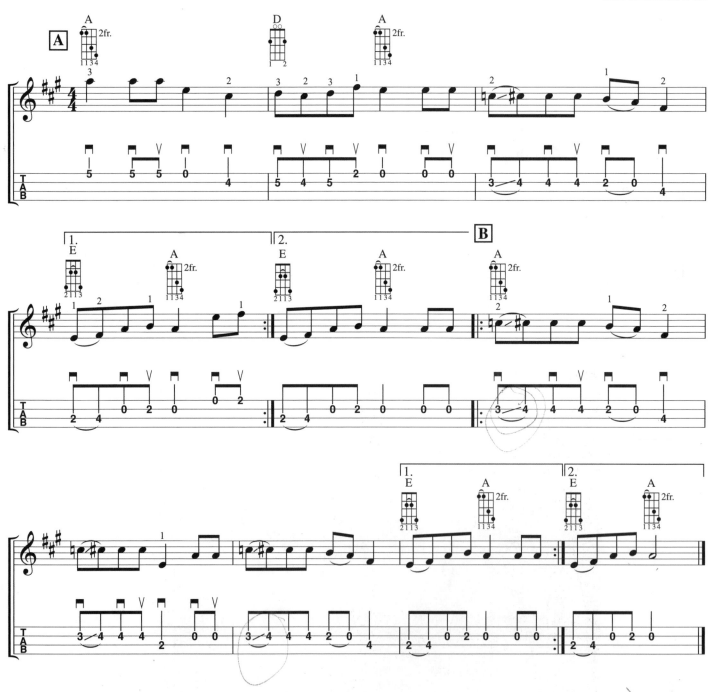

CRIPPLE CREEK
(Chord Progression)

TRADITIONAL

This arrangement of "Old Joe Clark" uses a variety of patterns and embellishments and has a real bluegrass sound. This tune is in the key of A, but the melody uses a G note (3rd fret of the 1st string) instead of the regular G♯ (4th fret of the 1st string) usually found in an A scale. This altered scale is called the *Mixolydian* mode in music theory and is actually a very common scale found in many old-time and bluegrass tunes. The first two notes of the tune are called "pickup" notes and happen on beat 4 before the actual downbeat of the tune. Count "1, 2, 3" and then play "4&":

OLD JOE CLARK

TRADITIONAL

OLD JOE CLARK
(Chord Progression)

TRADITIONAL

Congratulations! If you can play "Old Joe Clark," then you are well on your way toward becoming a bluegrass mandolin player.

Example 43: Sally Goodin

Here is another bluegrass jam favorite. Once again this is in AABB form. This tune has some hammer-ons, pull-offs, and lots of alternate picking. Watch your pick direction and count.

SALLY GOODIN

TRADITIONAL

Example 44: Sally Goodin (chord progression)

The chords are the same for both Section A and Section B of this tune.

SALLY GOODIN
(Chord Progression)

TRADITIONAL

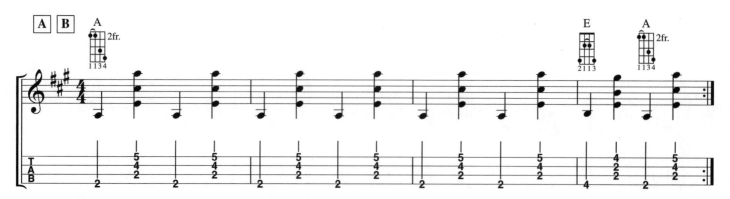

UNIT 5: BLUEGRASS RHYTHM CHOP

Up to now, we've been playing the chord changes to our tunes using basic chord shapes that involve open strings. This style of rhythm playing produces an open ringing sound that is similar to what a bluegrass guitarist might play. Bill Monroe, the father of bluegrass music, developed a different style in the mid-1940s. In this style, you use closed chord positions that have no open strings. Because there are no open strings, it is possible to shorten the ring of the chord and create a percussive backbeat strum commonly known as a rhythm "chop." This rhythm style supplies much of the driving beat in bluegrass music.

Here is the basic left-hand shape for a chop G chord:

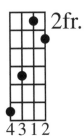

To create the proper bluegrass rhythm, play the chord on beats 2 and 4 and rest on beats 1 and 3, as in Example 45.

Example 45

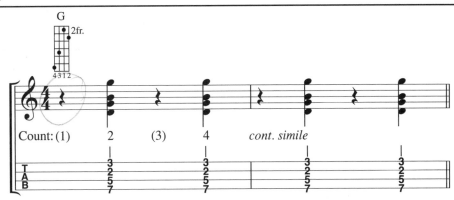

Try to make the chord chops on beats 2 and 4 short and percussive. To achieve this effect, strum the chord and then release your left hand just enough to stop the ringing of the chord. Don't take your fingers completely off the strings—maintain the shape of the chord with your left hand. This takes some practice. When done correctly, it will look almost like you are squeezing and releasing your left hand on the neck with each chord chop. Here's the chop position for a C chord—avoid playing the 1st string.

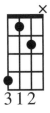

The D chord is just like the C chord position moved up two frets—avoid playing the 1st string.

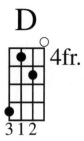

Here's an A chord (like the G chord moved up two frets).

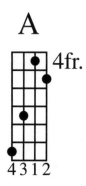

And an E chord (D chord moved up two frets).

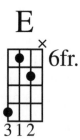

Now we have all the chop chord shapes we need to play the songs we've already learned. Remember, you can hear these mandolin chop parts in detail on the CD by panning the full band arrangement tracks hard right to isolate the mandolin.

BOIL THE CABBAGE DOWN
(Chord Chops)

TRADITIONAL

Example 47: Cumberland Gap (chop chords)

CUMBERLAND GAP
(Chord Chops)

TRADITIONAL

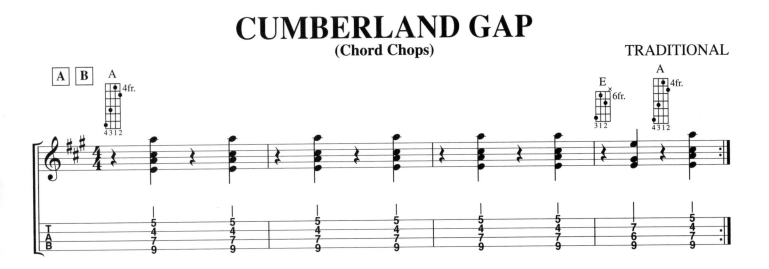

Example 48: Cripple Creek (chop chords)

CRIPPLE CREEK
(Chord Chops)

TRADITIONAL

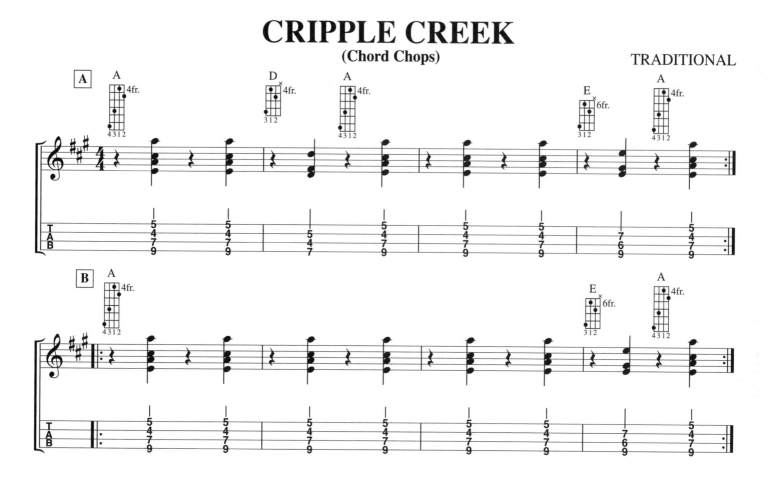

Example 49: Old Joe Clark (chop chords)

OLD JOE CLARK
(Chord Chops)

TRADITIONAL

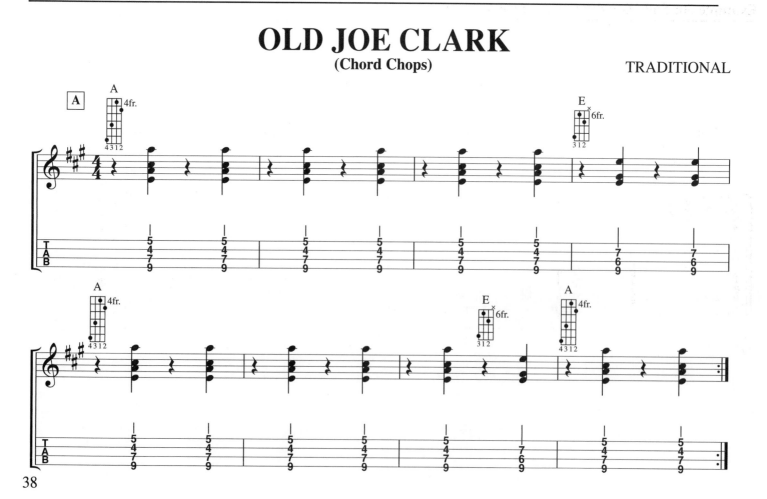

Example 50: Sally Goodin (chop chords)

SALLY GOODIN
(Chord Chops)

TRADITIONAL

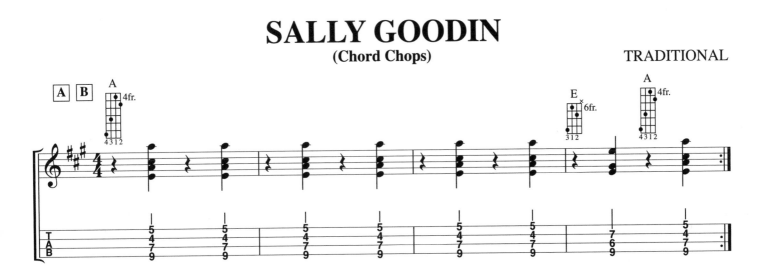

UNIT 6:
COMBINING TECHNIQUES AND MOVING UP THE NECK

Let's move on to a few tunes that use all the techniques you've learned up to now, with some new twists and turns thrown in to make things interesting. You will notice that from now on, the right-hand patterns used will be less repetitive and the use of left-hand ornaments will become more prominent. This is all part of the "right hand being a slave to the left" idea described earlier.

Example 51: Salt Creek

"Salt Creek" is another popular tune in AABB form—just follow the repeat signs. This tune is in the key of A, and, like "Old Joe Clark," it uses a G note in the melody (Mixolydian mode). Section B has some tricky rhythms, so be sure to count correctly and watch your pick direction.

SALT CREEK

40

SALT CREEK
(Chord Progression)

TRADITIONAL

FINGERBOARD POSITIONS

We need to briefly discuss the concept of fingerboard positions on the mandolin. The idea of "positioning" your left hand on the fingerboard comes from classical violin technique and stems from the need to organize the neck in some sort of pattern. Obviously, you won't always be playing with your left hand down close to the nut. Sometimes the music will require that you move up the neck to get higher notes, or perhaps play a passage in an area of the neck where the notes are easier to get. Here is the basic idea of positions on the mandolin: when your left-hand index finger is on the 1st or 2nd fret you are in "1st position." When you move your left hand up so that your index finger is on the 3rd or 4th fret, you are in "2nd position." When you move up still further so that your index finger is on the 5th or 6th fret, you are in "3rd position." There are many more positions, but you get the idea. So far, we have stayed in 1st position. In this book, we will be playing in 1st, 2nd, and 3rd positions.

KEY OF D

Now, let's move on to the key of D. The D scale looks like this.

Example 53

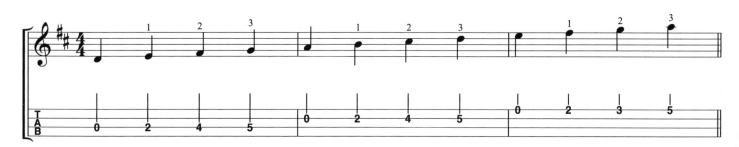

The scale above covers one octave and four notes, up to a high A on the 5th fret of the 1st string. In order to complete a two-octave scale, we need to shift out of 1st position and into "3rd position." Anchor your left-hand index finger on the 5th fret of the 1st string (A note) and leave it there while playing the last four notes of the scale (A, B, C♯, D). Use your pinky finger to get the high D note.

Example 54

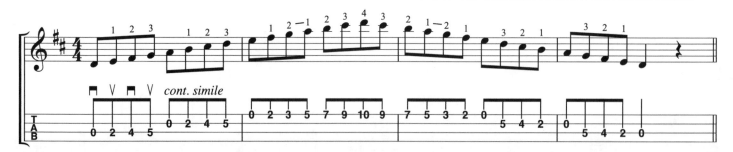

Even though we won't be shifting into 3rd position on the next tune, practicing this two-octave D scale is a great exercise. Practice this scale up and down, over and over.

Here's another bluegrass jam favorite. Watch out for your pick direction, especially in the A section—this particular string crossing pattern can be tricky at first. In section B, you'll need to use your left pinky finger to get the high B note on the 7th fret of the 1st string.

SOLDIER'S JOY

TRADITIONAL

The three main chords in the key of D are D, G, and A.

SOLDIER'S JOY
(Chord Progression)

TRADITIONAL

Example 57: Whiskey Before Breakfast

Here's a great Irish-sounding tune, "Whiskey Before Breakfast." This is another very popular jamming tune, and is usually played at a medium tempo. All of the notes in this melody are taken from the D scale.

WHISKEY BEFORE BREAKFAST

TRADITIONAL

In order to play the chords to "Whiskey Before Breakfast" we need to learn a new chord: E minor. Here's what an E minor chord looks like:

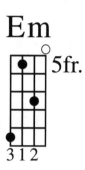

Notice that the E minor chord shape above looks almost like E major.

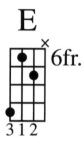

The only difference between E major and E minor chords is that you need to lower the position of your left-hand index finger by one fret for the minor chord.

WHISKEY BEFORE BREAKFAST
(Chord Progression)

TRADITIONAL

Example 59: John Henry

All of the tunes we've learned up to now are old fiddle tunes. While most of them have words, they are rarely sung in a bluegrass context. This next tune has many verses and is very often performed as a vocal. "John Henry" tells the story of a steel-driving railroad man. This version is also in the key of D and has a neat bluesy sound. The tune is not in the AABB form and there are no repeats—just play it from top to bottom. There are lots of slides and pull-offs here so be sure to watch out for your pick direction and count.

JOHN HENRY

TRADITIONAL

JOHN HENRY
(Chord Progression)

TRADITIONAL

UNIT 7: TREMOLO

One of the most unique and dynamic techniques we use on the mandolin is tremolo. Tremolo is a very common right-hand technique used in Italian, Greek, and Russian music, as well as bluegrass. It can be fast or slow, loud or soft, and a controlled tremolo can add a great emotional element to your playing. The basic right-hand tremolo motion is exactly like the down and up picking that you're already using, only faster.

Example 61

Try playing a tremolo on the open 2nd string: start slowly and gradually speed up your right-hand motion until you can't go any faster, then gradually slow it back down. Keep your wrist loose.

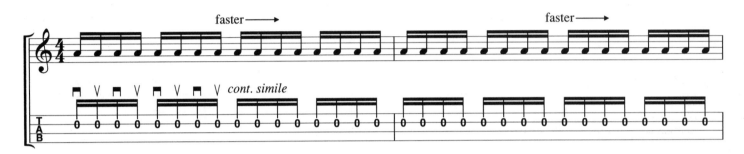

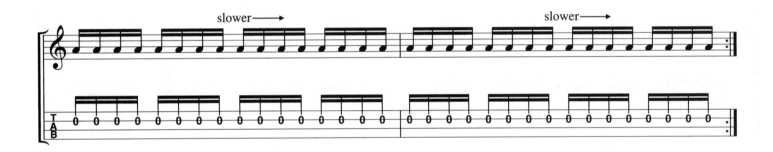

Be sure and listen to the CD to hear this effect. Notice that, as you speed up, the sound becomes more intense, and, as you slow down, it becomes more relaxed sounding. The goal is to be able to control the speed of the tremolo so you can control the level of intensity. This takes a lot of practice. It helps to start out playing softly—don't dig into the strings too much. Also, experiment with the distance of your right hand from the bridge. The string tension changes as you move away from the bridge and this can affect the ease of your tremolo. Remember to keep your right wrist loose!

Example 62

Now try the tremolo on the other open strings.

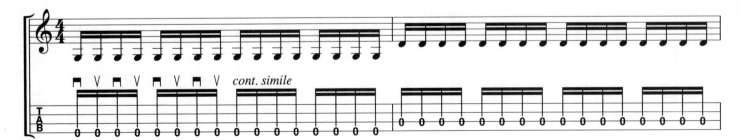

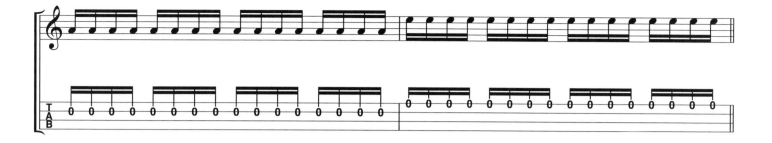

 Example 63

Once you begin to feel comfortable speeding up and slowing down your tremolo, try playing a G scale using the tremolo.

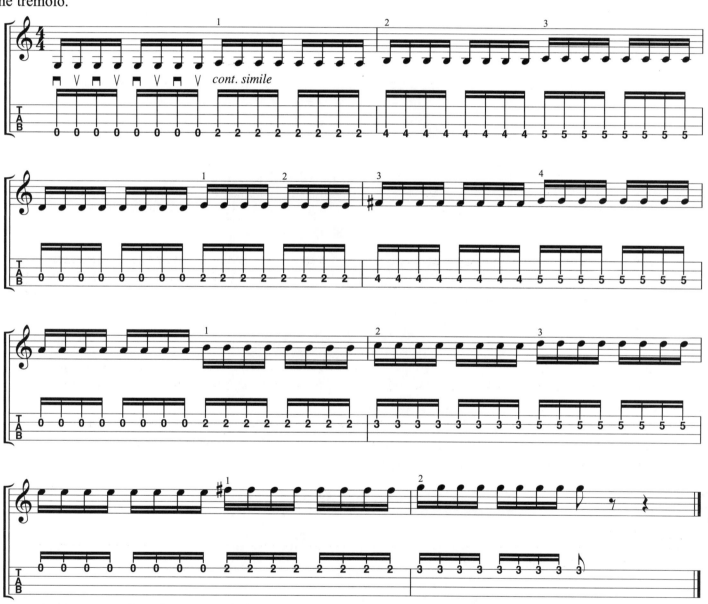

Notice that the tablature of example 63 shows you playing eight pick-strokes per scale tone. This is a good basic tremolo rate to aim for. Every player's tremolo is a bit different. As we said earlier, speeding up the tremolo increases the intensity and vice-versa. Experiment with different speeds to find out what works for you. Because tremolo consists of so many repeated notes, there is a different symbol for notating tremolo in music notation: 𝄒.

Example 64

A quarter-note tremolo indication means tremolo for one beat, a half note for two beats, etc.
Try practicing your tremolo using all of the scales you know. Practice, practice, practice!

WALTZ ($\frac{3}{4}$) TIME

Everything you've learned so far has been in $\frac{4}{4}$ time, also called *common time*, four beats to a measure. Many tunes in the bluegrass repertoire are in $\frac{3}{4}$, or waltz time, where there are only three beats per measure. This next song is an old gospel tune called "Amazing Grace." This tune is also in the key of D. We will be using the notes from a D scale to play the melody, and we'll also use lots of tremolo. Since you're in a new time signature ($\frac{3}{4}$), pay special attention to your counting and pick direction. Even though you're still using some of the same right-hand picking patterns you're already familiar with, they somehow feel different when playing in $\frac{3}{4}$ time. Notice the grouping of three notes together in several places—these are called "triplets" and are a division of the beat into three notes instead of two. Triplets are counted "1 trip-let. 2 trip-let, 3 trip-let." In this tune, the first two notes of the triplet are a pull-off so watch your pick direction closely and listen to the CD to hear how they should sound.

Example 65: Amazing Grace

Example 66

Playing rhythm in ¾ time is a little different than in 4/4 time. Here is the basic rhythm pattern for a D chord.

Example 67: Amazing Grace (chord progression)

AMAZING GRACE
(Chord Progression)

TRADITIONAL

UNIT 8: TWO CLASSIC BLUEGRASS STANDARDS

KEY OF C

 Example 68

Let's learn a little about the key of C. Here are the notes in the low octave C scale.

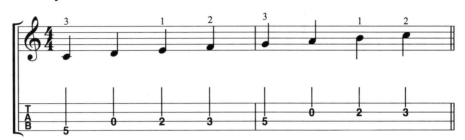

 Example 69

Here is the high octave C scale, which starts with your left-hand index finger on the 3rd fret of the 2nd string (this is "2nd position").

 Example 70

Here are both octaves together.

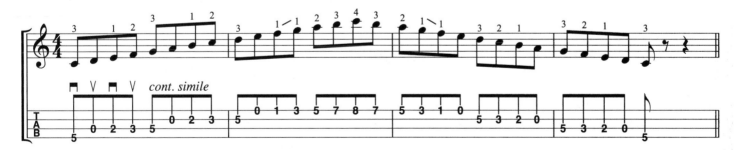

Practice this scale up and down, over and over, just like you did with your other scales.

The three main chords in the key of C are C, F, and G. Here are two different ways to make an F chord:

 Example 71: Wildwood Flower

Now let's try a tune in the key of C. "Wildwood Flower" is an old Carter Family tune and a bluegrass guitar favorite. This arrangement uses some "double stops." A double stop is two notes played simultaneously with one pick stroke (see measure 1). Also, notice the tremolo picking in the first part of the B Section. This passage is a little tricky—it starts in 2nd position with your ring finger on the 7th fret of the 2nd string (measure 11). In measure 13, you shift positions up to 3rd position with your middle finger on the 7th fret of the 3rd string, then reach up to get the 10th fret note with your pinky finger. There is a neat bluesy Bill Monroe-style lick in the last two measures.

56

WILDWOOD FLOWER

TRADITIONAL

57

WILDWOOD FLOWER
(Chord Progression)

TRADITIONAL

Example 73: John Hardy

Quite a number of the songs that have become instrumental bluegrass standards come from old-time Appalachian mountain music. In fact, just about every tune in this book falls into that category and many of them have lyrics. "John Hardy" tells the story of an outlaw on the run. (See lyrics on next page.)

There are three pickup notes out front—beat 1 is a rest, and you start playing the first pickup note on beat 2. This tune is in the key of G but the melody includes some F notes as well as F♯ notes. There are some more double stops here as well as some great bluesy licks.

JOHN HARDY

TRADITIONAL

John Hardy was a desperate little man
He wore his guns every day
He shot down a man on the West Virginia line
You should've seen John Hardy getting away, oh Lord,
You should've seen John Hardy getting away.

Example 74: John Hardy (chord progression)

JOHN HARDY
(Chord Progression)

TRADITIONAL

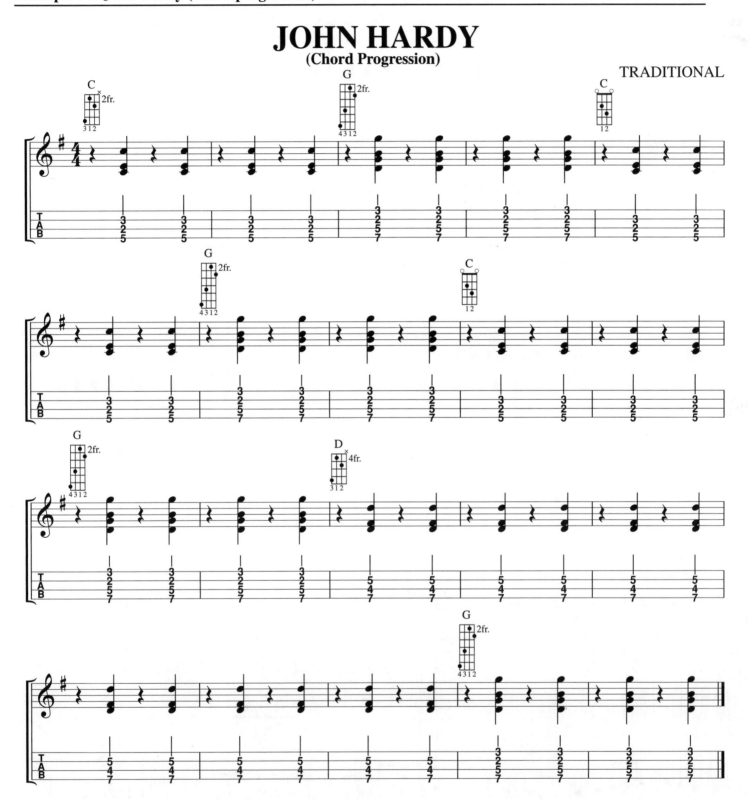

UNIT 9: DEVELOPING YOUR RIGHT HAND

The most difficult part of learning to flatpick is developing a good right hand. Many bluegrass tunes are played at a fast tempo—some are very fast—and developing speed is necessary to play these tunes in a band context. However, playing cleanly is more important than playing fast, especially when you are starting out. Speed comes by practicing precisely and getting rid of any sloppiness in your playing. Here are some exercises to help develop the speed and accuracy of your right hand—pay close attention to your pick direction.

Example 75

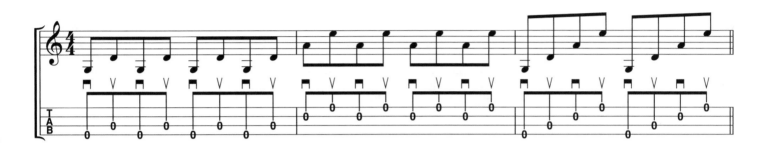

Example 76

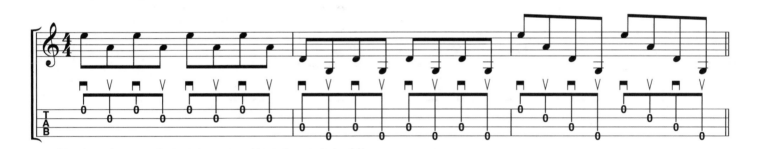

Example 77

Here is a pattern commonly used by drummers called a "paradiddle."

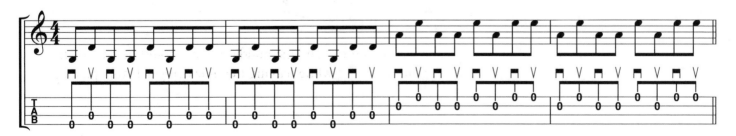

Example 78

This pattern places the accent on every third note—watch your pick direction.

Using that same idea of a repeating pattern of three notes, but spread out across three strings—this is commonly called "crosspicking"—we will use this pattern later in a tune.

Example 79

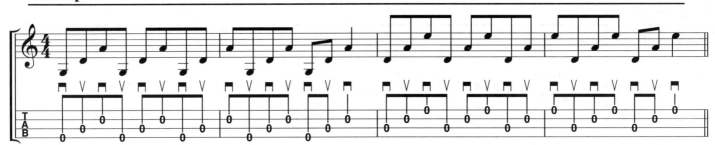

Here is a syncopated pattern that leaves out every third note—be sure to count and watch your pick direction.

Example 80

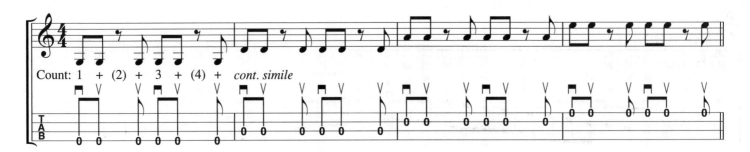

Count: 1 + (2) + 3 + (4) + *cont. simile*

These are just a few of the infinite possibilities for right-hand picking exercises. Practice these over and over and see if you can come up with some variations of your own as well.

62

UNIT 10: DEVELOPING YOUR LEFT HAND

Strengthening the muscles in your left hand will improve your ability to fret notes cleanly and play faster and with more coordination. Usually the index and middle fingers are the strongest, with the ring and pinky fingers needing more work. These exercises will help to strengthen all your fingers.

Example 81

Here is a G scale with one open string—use your pinky finger to get the notes of the other open strings instead.

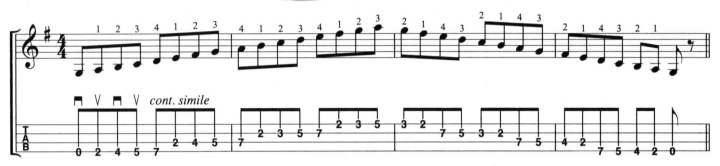

Example 82

A C scale using the pinky.

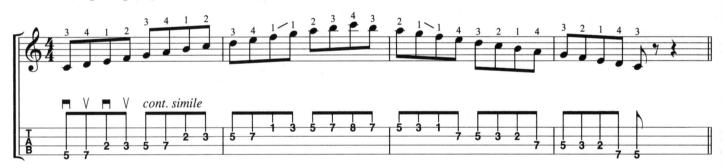

Example 83

A D scale.

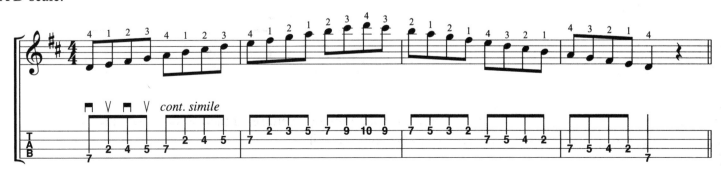

Example 84

And an A scale.

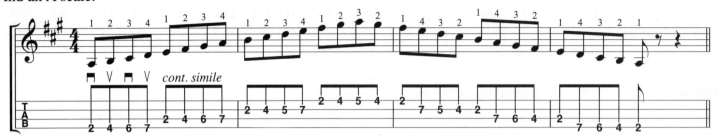

Unlike the scales above, these next exercises are not necessarily meant to sound good—they are strictly for strengthening your fingers.

Example 85

Anchor your first finger and leave it down while you alternate between your other fingers.

Example 86

Try these 1–3 and 2–4 finger combinations.

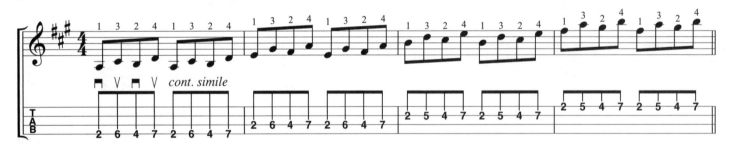

Example 87

Here's one that reminds me of a spider crawling over the fretboard.

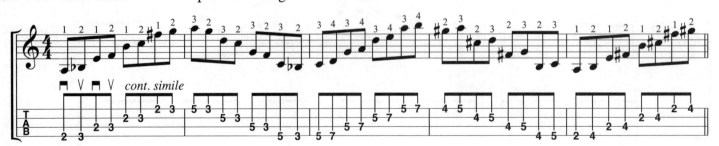

Example 88: Salt Creek Section B (up the neck)

Here's an alternate B Section for "Salt Creek" that shifts between 3rd and 2nd positions. To play the lick in the first two measures, anchor your index finger at the 5th fret on the 1st string (3rd position) and leave it down while you play the lick. In measures 3–4, the hand position is the same, but moved down two frets (2nd position) to play over the G chord. Licks that are movable like this are called "closed position" licks because they use no open strings and are totally movable around the neck. This lick uses the "paradiddle" right-hand picking pattern described in the preceding exercises.

SALT CREEK
(Up the Neck)

TRADITIONAL

65

ENDINGS

Here are two different endings that you can use for tunes in the key of A. Both of these are the same length—four measures. This is known as a "double shave and a haircut."

Example 89

This is a fiddle tune-style ending that would be good for "Boil the Cabbage Down" or "Cripple Creek."

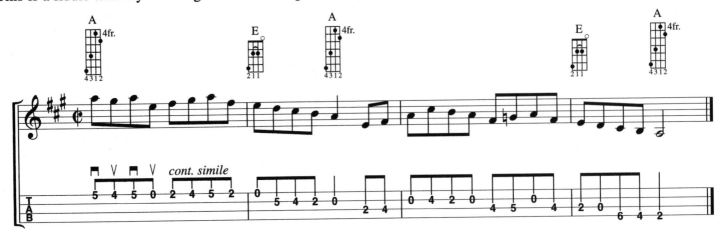

Example 90

This one is a little more bluesy and is good for "Old Joe Clark" or "Salt Creek."

UNIT 11 : MORE ADVANCED TUNES

60

Example 91: Lonesome Road Blues

Here is a very popular bluegrass tune, especially among banjo players. This tune is usually played pretty fast. This version is in G, but uses some bluesy notes not found in the normal G scale.

LONESOME ROAD BLUES

TRADITIONAL

LONESOME ROAD BLUES
(Chord Progression)

TRADITIONAL

This old southern anthem makes a great bluegrass tune. Watch your pick direction and count.

DIXIE

TRADITIONAL

70

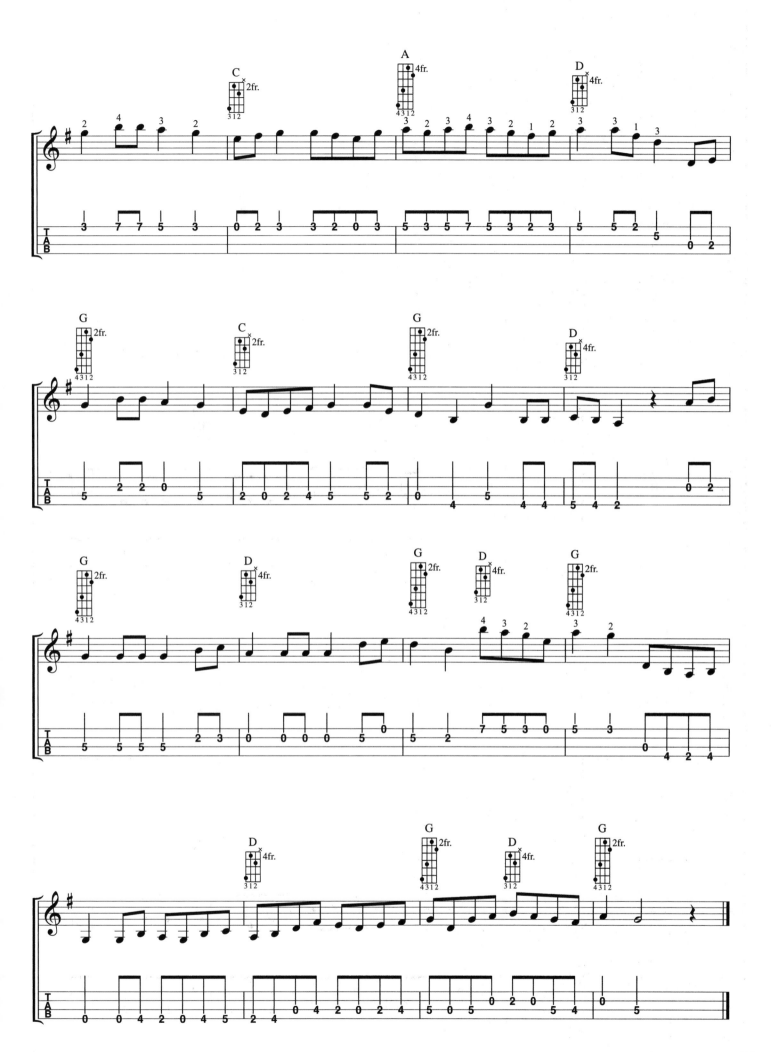

DIXIE
(Chord Progression)

TRADITIONAL

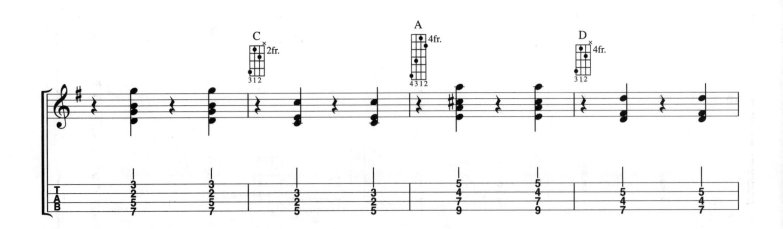

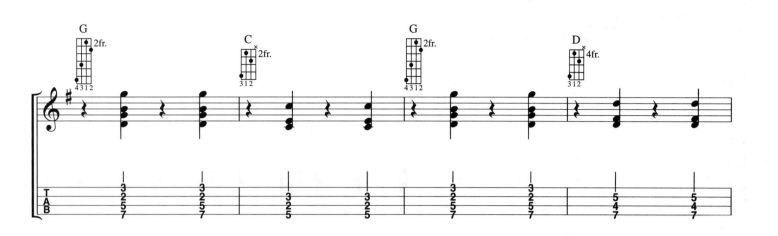

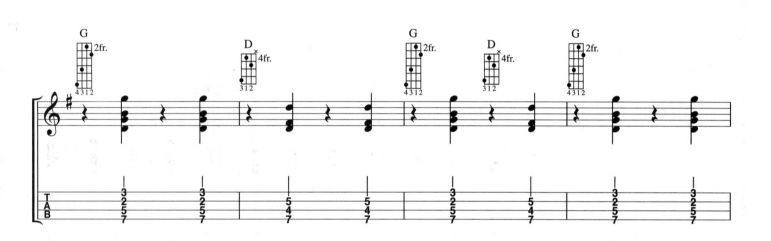

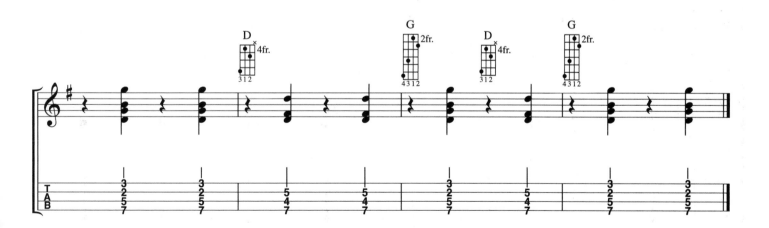

Example 95: Blackberry Blossom

This is probably the all-time favorite melodic jam tune for bluegrass players. The A section is in the key of G, and the B section is in E minor. This tune has a great melody and a very active chord progression (especially in the A section). In the second B section, pay special attention to your pick direction during the triplet lick in measure 4. This is a hammer on followed by a pull-off, all done with one downstroke of the pick.

BLACKBERRY BLOSSOM

TRADITIONAL

74

Example 96: Blackberry Blossom (chord progression)

In order to play the backup for "Blackberry Blossom," we need a B chord. Here are two ways to make a B chord.

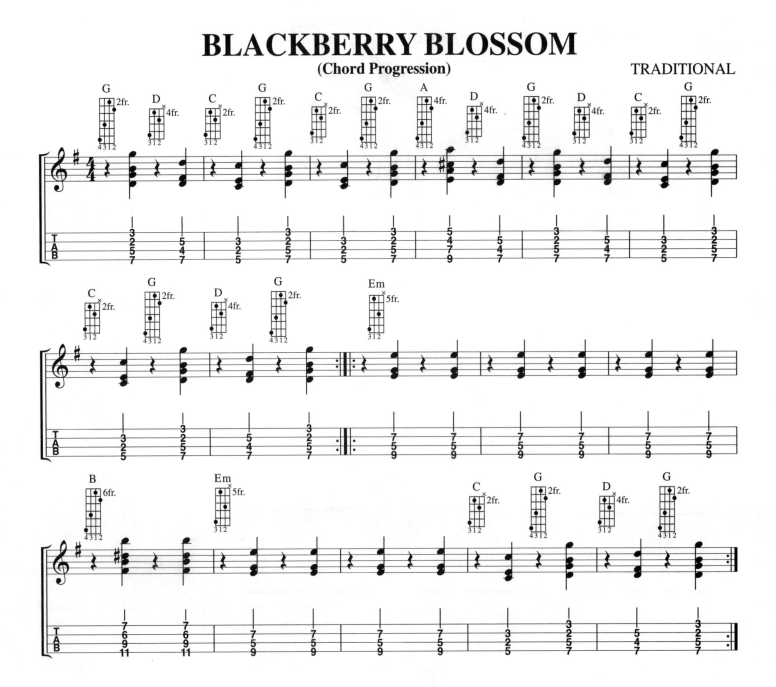

Example 97: Black Mountain Rag

"Black Mountain Rag" is an old fiddle tune that has become a flatpicking standard in bluegrass. It was originally recorded by the legendary guitarist Doc Watson, one of the pioneers of solo guitar flatpicking. There are three sections to this tune, with sections A and B both having the same chord progression. For this reason, it can be tricky to play backup along with this one; only section C (3rd section) goes to the D chord. Also in section C, notice the "crosspicking" right-hand pattern. Pay attention to your pick direction and count.

BLACK MOUNTAIN RAG

TRADITIONAL

78

BLACK MOUNTAIN RAG
(Chord Progression)

TRADITIONAL

CD SONG LIST FOR FULL BAND ARRANGEMENTS

The following is a list of the band tunes on the CD. After each title, you will find the key in which the tune is being played. Also included is the order of solos for the tune. The arrangements will give you the feel of playing in a jam session or band context. Whichever instrument takes the first solo also takes the last solo and will end the tune. The mandolin follows the tablature in the book, for both solos and backup. Remember, if you want to remove the mandolin from the mix and hear just the other instruments in the band, pan the music hard left. To hear only the mandolin, pan hard right.

Boil the Cabbage Down: Key of A
Solos: fiddle, banjo, mandolin, guitar, fiddle

Cripple Creek: Key of A
Solos: banjo, fiddle, mandolin, guitar, banjo

Old Joe Clark: Key of A
Solos: fiddle, banjo, mandolin, guitar, fiddle

Salt Creek: Key of A
Solos: banjo, fiddle, mandolin, guitar, banjo

John Henry: Key of D
Solos: guitar, banjo, mandolin, fiddle, guitar

John Hardy: Key of G
Solos: guitar, banjo, mandolin, fiddle, guitar

Wildwood Flower: Key of C
Solos: guitar, banjo, mandolin, fiddle, guitar

Sally Goodin: Key of A
Solos: fiddle, banjo, mandolin, guitar, fiddle

Cumberland Gap: Key of A
Solos: banjo, fiddle, mandolin, guitar, banjo

Lonesome Road Blues: Key of G
Solos: banjo, fiddle, mandolin, guitar, banjo

Amazing Grace: Key of D
Solos: mandolin, fiddle, banjo, guitar, mandolin

Soldier's Joy: Key of D
Solos: fiddle, banjo, mandolin, guitar, fiddle

Whiskey Before Breakfast: Key of D
Solos: mandolin, guitar, fiddle, banjo, mandolin

Blackberry Blossom: Key of G
Solos: guitar, fiddle, mandolin, banjo, guitar

Dixie: Key of G
Solos: banjo, mandolin, guitar, fiddle, banjo

Black Mountain Rag: Key of A
Solos: guitar, fiddle, mandolin, banjo, guitar

APPENDIX 1

Reading Music Notation

Music is written on a **staff.** The staff consists of five lines and four spaces between the lines:

The names of the notes are the same as the first seven letters of the alphabet: A B C D E F G.

The notes are written in alphabetical order. The first (lowest) line is E:

Notes can extend above and below the staff. When they do, **ledger lines** are added. Here is the approximate range of the mandolin from the lowest note, open 4th string G to a B on the 1st string at the 19th fret.

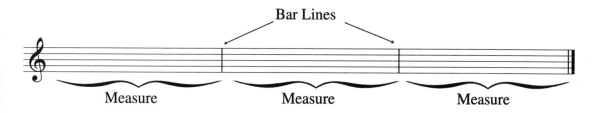

The staff is divided into **measures** by **bar lines.** A heavy double bar line marks the end of the music.

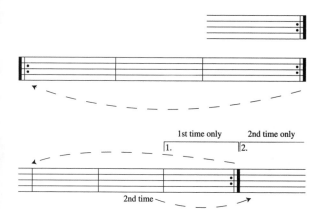

The repeat sign looks like a double barline, with two dots positioned in the spaces above and below the center line of the staff. With multiple endings, a repeat sign is placed at the beginning of the section and at the last barline of the 1st ending.

APPENDIX 2

Rhythm Notation and Time Signatures

At the beginning of every song is a time signature. $\frac{4}{4}$ is the most common time signature.

$\frac{4}{4}$ FOUR COUNTS TO A MEASURE

A QUARTER NOTE RECEIVES ONE COUNT

The top number tells you how many counts per measure.
The bottom number tells you which kind of note receives one count.

The time value of a note is determined by three things:

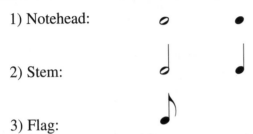

1) Notehead:

2) Stem:

3) Flag:

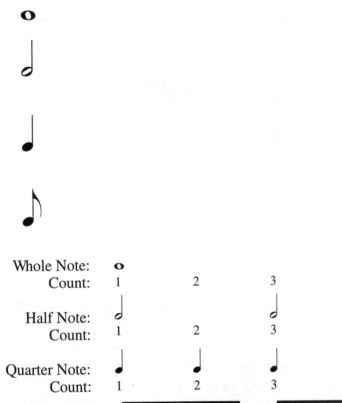

Whole Note:	o			
Count:	1	2	3	4
Half Note:	♩		♩	
Count:	1	2	3	4
Quarter Note:	♩	♩	♩	♩
Count:	1	2	3	4
Eighth Note:	♪ ♪	♪ ♪	♪ ♪	♪ ♪
Count:	1 +	2 +	3 +	4 +

Count out loud and clap the rhythm to this excerpt from "Jingle Bells."

Four counts per measure

84   A Quarter Note Receives One Count

APPENDIX 3

Reading Tablature and Fingerboard Diagrams

Tablature (TAB) illustrates the location of notes on the neck of the mandolin. This illustration compares the four strings of a mandolin with the four lines of tablature.

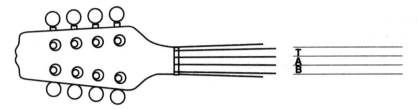

 Notes are indicated by placing fret numbers on the strings. A "0" represents an open string.

This tablature indicates to play the open, 1st, and 3rd frets on the first string.

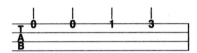

Tablature is usually used in conjunction with standard music notation. The rhythms and note names are indicated by the standard notation, and the location of those notes on the mandolin neck is indicated by the tablature.

Chords are often indicated in chord block diagrams. In these diagrams, vertical lines represent the strings; the vertical line on the left represents the 4th string, the second line from the left represents the 3rd string, etc. The horizontal lines represent the frets; a thick horizontal line across the top of the vertical lines represents the nut of the instrument in open position. A number followed by the abbreviation "fr." to the right of the diagram denotes the position of the lowest fret depicted in the diagram. A circle above any of the vertical lines represents an open string. Black dots on the diagram represent left-hand fingers on the fingerboard. Numbers beneath the diagram indicate the left-hand finger employed on the string immediately above. 1 = index finger, 2 = middle finger, 3 = ring finger, 4 = pinky.

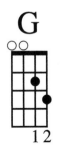

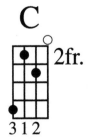

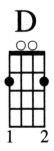

ABOUT THE AUTHOR

Dennis Caplinger is a multi-talented musician who has toured and recorded with many different artists including Bluegrass Etc., Eric Clapton, Vince Gill, Nickel Creek, Chris Hillman, Herb Pedersen, Byron Berline, Dan Crary, Richard Greene, Chris Thile, Sean Watkins, John Reischman, Ray Park, Jann Browne, Kevin Welch, Kelly Willis, Ray Price, Rita Coolidge, Buck Howdy, Tim Flannery, Eve Selis, and The Academy of Country Music Awards Show Band. His busy touring schedule as banjoist/fiddler with Bluegrass Etc. has taken him all over the world and yielded three critically acclaimed albums to date; their latest, *Home Is Where the Heart Is,* was voted one of the top ten bluegrass recordings of the year for 1999 by the *Chicago Tribune.* A highly sought-after player/producer in the West Coast studio scene, he has worked on countless jingles, commercials, cartoons, and movies and has his own production company based in Vista, California. Dennis is actively producing and playing on projects for CMH records' popular *Pickin' On* series. Featured records he has been a part of include tributes to Eric Clapton, Santana, Creed, the Rolling Stones, Led Zeppelin, Bonnie Raitt, Jim Morrison, Queen, Neil Diamond, Dave Matthews Band, R.E.M., ZZ Top, Lynyrd Skynyrd, the Black Crowes, Phish, Dolly Parton, Brooks and Dunn, Lonestar, Lee Ann Womack, Jo Dee Messina, Tim McGraw, Montgomery Gentry, Keith Urban, Tracy Byrd, LeAnn Rimes, Indigo Girls, Rod Stewart, and Nancy Sinatra. His movie soundtrack credits include *Back to the Future III, El Diablo, Rio Diablo,* Steven King's *Apt Pupil,* and the current HBO series "Deadwood," among others. Dennis's playing is featured on the soundtrack of "The Simpsons" and Warner Bros. cartoons "Pinky and the Brain" and "Histeria," as well as numerous programs on PBS, A&E, TNN, and The History Channel. Recent commercials include those for New York Life, Supercuts, Subway, The Home Depot, St. Joseph's Aspirin, Applebee's, Discover Card featuring John Lithgow, and Cingular Wireless, which Dennis appeared along with Bluegrass Etc. Dennis has contributed to *Banjo Newsletter* and can be seen in the October 1999 issue of *Bluegrass Now* magazine, which contains a feature article on him.